Visit and Learn
Alcatraz

by Tamika M. Murray

FOCUS READERS®
BEACON

www.focusreaders.com

Copyright © 2024 by Focus Readers®, Lake Elmo, MN 55042. All rights reserved. No part of this book may be reproduced or utilized in any form or by any means without written permission from the publisher.

Focus Readers is distributed by North Star Editions:
sales@northstareditions.com | 888-417-0195

Produced for Focus Readers by Red Line Editorial.

Photographs ©: Shutterstock Images, cover, 1, 4, 7, 11, 17, 20–21, 22, 25, 26, 29; Detroit Photographic Co./Library of Congress, 8; Ernest King/AP Images, 13; AP Images, 14; Robert W. Klein/AP Images, 19

Library of Congress Cataloging-in-Publication Data
Library of Congress Cataloging-in-Publication Data is available on the Library of Congress website.

ISBN
978-1-63739-614-8 (hardcover)
978-1-63739-671-1 (paperback)
978-1-63739-781-7 (ebook pdf)
978-1-63739-728-2 (hosted ebook)

Printed in the United States of America
Mankato, MN
082023

About the Author

Tamika M. Murray is an award-winning author of nonfiction books and a Trending News Writer for Delishably.com. She currently resides in Southern New Jersey with her three rambunctious kitties.

Table of Contents

CHAPTER 1
High Security 5

CHAPTER 2
From Fort to Prison 9

CHAPTER 3
Life on Alcatraz 15

Escape! 20

CHAPTER 4
Behind the Walls 23

Focus on Alcatraz • 28
Glossary • 30
To Learn More • 31
Index • 32

Chapter 1

High Security

The sun shines on San Francisco Bay. Crowds of people gather into lines. The cold wind stings their faces. A girl observes seagulls diving for food. Then she sees a lighthouse off in the distance.

Several ferries go to Alcatraz every day.

Soon, the line moves toward a **ferry**. Everyone walks aboard.

The ferry takes them to Alcatraz Island. This island is different from the other islands in the bay. It was once home to a prison. The US government ran it from 1934 to 1963. The prison had very high security. It held many **inmates**.

Alcatraz housed famous inmates such as Al Capone.

 Alcatraz Island is approximately 1.5 miles (2.4 km) from the city of San Francisco.

Escape was nearly impossible. That is part of the reason why the prison was built on an island.

Chapter 2

From Fort to Prison

Alcatraz Island is in California. It got its name from a Spanish explorer. In 1775, he sailed into San Francisco Bay. He named one of the islands Alcatraces. Later, the name changed to Alcatraz.

 Alcatraz Island was controlled by the Ohlone people before Spain took over the area.

In 1848, California became part of the United States. Two years later, the US president set aside Alcatraz Island. He made it a military area.

Soon, a **fort** was built there. Much of the fort was made of wood. The army put many large guns on the

Alcatraces is a Spanish word for a type of seabird. Many seabirds live near the island.

 The lighthouse on Alcatraz was built in 1854. It was the first lighthouse on the West Coast.

island. The fort protected the city of San Francisco.

Fort Point and Lime Point were nearby. They guarded the area, too.

All three forts worked together. They helped keep the bay safe.

The army used Alcatraz as a military prison. The fort held prisoners from the US Civil War (1861–1865). Prisoners from later wars also stayed on the island.

In the 1910s, the prison was rebuilt. Workers used concrete instead of wood. Fire was now less of a risk. The prison also got a new nickname. People called it "The Rock."

 A photo from 1933 shows the prison's laundry room, power plant, and storage room.

By 1933, the army no longer needed Alcatraz as a military prison. So, the US government took control of the island.

Chapter 3

Life on Alcatraz

In 1934, Alcatraz became a **federal** prison. Workers updated the buildings. They made Alcatraz harder to escape. It became one of the strongest prisons in the United States.

Warden James A. Johnston points to one of the new cells in 1934.

James A. Johnston served as the first **warden** of Alcatraz. He hired one guard for every three inmates. Each inmate had his own **cell**. Many inmates had done violent crimes. Some were bank robbers. Others had kidnapped or killed people.

A few inmates were famous. One was Alvin Karpowicz. He led a **gang** for many years. Karpowicz spent more than 25 years on the island. That's longer than any other inmate at Alcatraz.

 Alcatraz had 378 cells, but the prison was never full.

The government grew concerned about Alcatraz in the late 1950s. Repair costs were high. Running the prison cost a lot, too. Food and supplies had to be shipped in.

17

And shipping was expensive. It cost $10 per day to house each inmate. At other prisons, the cost was only $3 per day. So, in 1963, the government closed Alcatraz.

The prison sat empty for several years. But in 1972, Alcatraz became part of the National Park Service.

Did You Know?

Alcatraz was a federal prison for 29 years. During that time, it housed 1,576 inmates.

 When Alcatraz closed, guards moved the inmates to other prisons.

Visitors could now tour the island. By 1986, Alcatraz was named a historic **landmark**.

THAT'S AMAZING!

Escape!

Three inmates tried to escape Alcatraz in 1962. First, the men secretly made holes in their walls. Next, they made fake heads. They left the heads on their pillows at night. Then they crawled through the holes. The guards saw the fake heads. They thought the men were sleeping.

The inmates reached the roof. Then they slid down a pipe. Finally, the men cut a fence. They reached the water. They set out on a raft made of raincoats. The inmates were never seen again. But a raft and paddle were found on a nearby island.

A display shows one of the fake heads and a hole in the wall.

Chapter 4

Behind the Walls

Alcatraz is now a popular **tourist** attraction. Large crowds gather every day. People take ferries to reach Alcatraz. Some people go on helicopter tours. They view the island from above.

 A crowd gathers on Alcatraz Island after getting off the ferry.

Visitors can do many activities at Alcatraz. One **exhibit** is called the Big Lockup. Visitors look at pictures and text. The exhibit teaches the history of the island's time as a prison.

Many visitors tour the empty prison. Some people explore on their own. They see buildings where

More than 1.5 million people visit Alcatraz every year.

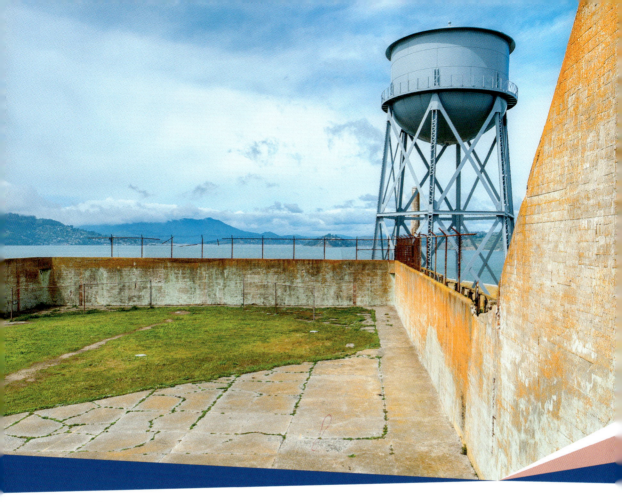

 Visitors can walk around the area where inmates exercised.

guards and inmates lived. They can also listen to audio on their phones. They hear guards and inmates talk about what the prison was like.

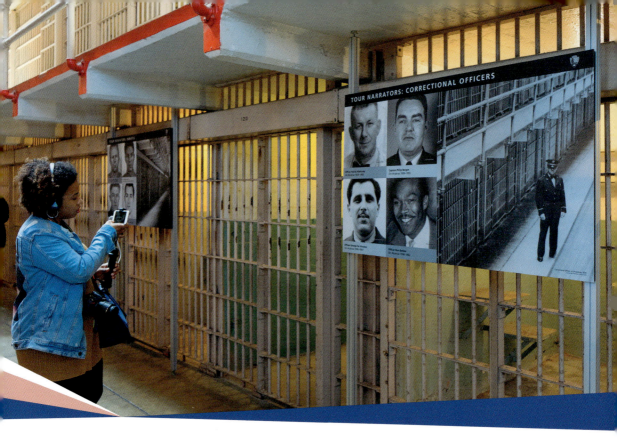

 Signs and audio guides help visitors learn about the prison.

Other visitors join a guided tour. The guide shows them around the island. The guide tells facts and stories. Visitors can choose from several types of tours. The Alcatraz

Behind the Scenes Tour takes about two hours. Visitors see hidden doorways and a tunnel. They also see an underground jail area.

Some visitors do the Alcatraz Night Tour. This tour includes sunset views of the Golden Gate Bridge. Visitors also see how a cell door works.

After the tour, visitors can explore the island. They can see gardens and a lighthouse. Alcatraz offers many ways to experience history.

FOCUS ON
Alcatraz

Write your answers on a separate piece of paper.

1. Write a sentence that describes the main ideas of Chapter 3.

2. Do you think the inmates who escaped Alcatraz lived? Why or why not?

3. What nickname was given to Alcatraz in the 1910s?
   - **A.** The Fort
   - **B.** The Rock
   - **C.** The Island

4. What could have happened if the prison was never changed from wood to concrete?
   - **A.** A flood could have happened.
   - **B.** A fight could have happened.
   - **C.** A fire could have happened.

5. What does **observes** mean in this book?

*A girl **observes** seagulls diving for food. Then she sees a lighthouse off in the distance.*

   A. runs from
   B. watches
   C. catches

6. What does **attraction** mean in this book?

*Alcatraz is now a popular tourist **attraction**. Large crowds gather every day.*

   A. something people want to see
   B. something people don't know about
   C. something people stay away from

Answer key on page 32.

Glossary

cell
A small room where a prisoner must stay.

exhibit
A public display of art or other items of interest.

federal
Having to do with the top level of government.

ferry
A boat used to move people, vehicles, or goods from one place to another.

fort
A protected building or area of land.

gang
A group that takes part in illegal behavior, sometimes using violence.

inmates
People who must stay in a prison.

landmark
A place or a building that is easily recognized.

tourist
A person who visits an area for fun or enjoyment.

warden
A person who is in charge of a prison.

To Learn More

BOOKS

Chandler, Matt. *Daring Escape From Alcatraz*. North Mankato, MN: Capstone Press, 2022.

Hansen, Grace. *History's Infamous Unsolved Crimes*. Minneapolis: Abdo Publishing, 2023.

Schwartz, Heather E. *Inside Alcatraz*. Minneapolis: Lerner Publications, 2023.

NOTE TO EDUCATORS

Visit **www.focusreaders.com** to find lesson plans, activities, links, and other resources related to this title.

Index

C
Capone, Al, 6
Civil War, 12

E
escape, 7, 15, 20
exhibits, 24

F
federal prison, 15, 18
ferry, 6, 23
fort, 10–12

I
inmates, 6, 16, 18, 20, 25

J
Johnston, James A., 16

K
Karpowicz, Alvin, 16

L
lighthouse, 5, 27

M
military prison, 12–13

N
National Park Service, 18

S
San Francisco Bay, 5–6, 9, 12

T
tours, 19, 23–27

Answer Key: 1. Answers will vary; **2.** Answers will vary; **3.** B; **4.** C; **5.** B; **6.** A